REFLE

PAIN IN T

Based on a True Story

A Journey of two orphans

By Evelyn T.S Nwaeze

REFLECTIONS
PAIN IN THE TUNNEL

By Evelyn T.S Nwaeze

Copyright

Copyright @ 2021 by Evelyn T.S. Nwaeze

Copyright filed with the Canadian Intellectual Property Office

All rights reserved, no part of this publication may be reproduced, distributed or transmitted in any form or means including photocopying, or other electronical or mechanical methods, without prior written permission of the publisher, except for quotation in critical reviews and certain other noncommercial uses permitted by copyright law. For permission request, email vaidastouch@gmail.com

Disclaimer: The stories in this book are based on true events, however, any reference to historical events, real people or real places have been changed by the author to preserve their identities. Any close resemblance to the actual persons, living or dead, events, or locales is entirely due to being part of the true story, their exclusion would jeopardize the trueness and completeness of these narratives.

Book Cover and design by Arash Jahani
www.arashjahani.com

Written by Evelyn T.S Nwaeze of Powell River, B.C, Canada

Published by Evelyn T.S Nwaeze:- KD Publishing

Email: vaidastouch@gmail.com

Dedications

To my Mom, my strength, my angel, I am who I am because of you. The lessons that you've given me are beyond priceless, for that I am greatly thankful.

To my Grandparents, your love was unconditional, and you taught me to have a 'Can do' attitude and that nothing was impossible.

To the loves of my life:

My Kids, Tanya, Alicia-Tyra, Jayden and Kendall. My precious gifts from God, I'm forever grateful and thankful for the Joy that you bring me.

And finally, Felix, the love of my life. My life partner, my Dim, my Mudiwa. Thank you for loving me wholly for who I am, my best friend, your love is unmatched, your support is motivating, may God continue to bless your beautiful soul my love.

Table of Contents

Copyright 3
Dedications..................................4
Preface 8
Chapter 1: **Now & Then: At Home & Grandma's House** 12
Chapter 2: **New Life & Life then, few months after.** 16
Chapter 3: **Sunset Cruising & Sister Chat** 22
Chapter 4: **Breakfast with Derek** 30
Chapter 5: **Lunch chatting with Romona** 34
Chapter 6: **Current life; triumphs & challenges** 41
Chapter 7: **The Outdoor Run** 48
Chapter 8: **The Subtle Joy** 56
Chapter 9: **The Therapist: Nice to Meet you** 62
Chapter 10: **The Project & First Signs of Hope.** 71
Chapter 11: **Therapy Session 4: Welcome back** 75

Chapter 12: *The Anticipation & The Setbacks* 79

Chapter 13: *The Thieving Saving Angel* 84

Chapter 14: **The rays of light** 96

Chapter 15: **The Working life & The Orphan title.** 103

Chapter 16: **The Worst is left Unwritten** 110

Chapter 17: *The beautiful blessings* 115

Chapter 18: *Adopted Mindset Now & the Future* 122

Epilogue: *The Pain of an Orphan The comfort and hope* 126

Acknowledgements 129

Bibliography: **References** 131

Preface

This book is written in real life reflection of actual events regarding how two young orphans had to navigate through life after losing their parents: the untold struggles of suffering through the process in the hopes for a better day. Their experience seeks to spur you into taking hold of your own life, irrespective of your past experiences.

Grab a coffee, wine or beer whichever rocks your boat and enjoy this read that allows you to have a glimpse of what it's like to go through the critical phase of life as struggling orphans.

Oftentimes, life does not serve us our desires, but regardless of what life offers, one must have the strength, resilience, endurance, patience and hope to turn it around.

Read on to find out what the two encountered along their journey, the trials and tribulations in hopes to see the light at the end of the tunnel.

REFLECTIONS

PAIN IN THE TUNNEL

EVELYN T.S NWAEZE

Chapter 1: *Now & Then: At Home & Grandma's House*

As Sarah sipped a glass of her favourite red wine, sitting on a swing chair by her partly shaded Pergola, the birds chirping away as if they were having a deep conversation with each other.

For a second she diverted her attention from her kids, who were screaming loudly with the joy of playing outside in the sun in their garden playhouse. Yes, it was such a gloriously orgasmic warm day, with the perfect temperature and ideal amount of breeze. 'Oh wow!!, another overwhelming thought of gratitude encompassed Sarah as she looked around her beautifully manicured yard, filled with blooming lavender flowers, loads of striving palm trees, with such relief and sigh at the same time, not sure whether it's a lovely feeling or it's yet another ailing reminder of the painful past.

As usual, Sarah tried to shrug off that mixed thought, she found herself slowly going back into, as if it had a magnetic pull effect on her. She occasionally has this thing lingering in her mind that constantly reminds her where she came from, like a scar embossed on her now ever so happy, fun filled life.

Fiddling with her rings, a quick glance at her kids scattered around the garden, she took another sip rather more like a gulp of the red wine, and stared into the space between the tall pine trees in the distance, and away she slipped back into her memory. She calls it the torment tunnel, of which each time she goes back that memory lane, it feels surreal, filled with excruciating pain and struggle, that still has an unbearable sting.

Yes, people often talk about the light at the end of the tunnel, and for most, although the light eventually comes, the pain lies within the walk. Sarah blinked slowly as she remembered the gruesome journey that she walked with her sister Nancy.

Nothing prepares anyone for the moment of receiving the saddest news one could ever receive of being told that their mother or father had just passed away.

As Sarah submerged herself into the ocean of thoughts, she found herself drifted way back to about a month after her Mum's passing.

Sarah remembers everybody returning to their usual day to day life, and the smiles starting to form on people's faces that were once covered in tears. The large people gathering was finally diminishing to only five to six people remaining. She remembers sitting by the veranda watching random people walk past her Grandma's house, as she kept wondering when they were going to go back home.

"Oh Wait!! Going back home? Who is going to be at home with us? Of course, Zillah will still be working for us, right? But how are we going to pay her? My older sister Nancy is only eighteen and I'm only sixteen. How is this gonna work? What about school? What's going to happen, I need to get a new school soon? At least Nancy is going to finish her last year in high school this year and go to college. I still have a few more years. What am I going to tell my friends who probably have no idea about my Mum's passing? At least some of them from our hometown Southertonville know about it, I saw them at the funeral. Oh gosh, my head is about to burst with flooding thoughts, but why did this happen to us? I can't believe Mum is gone, like gone, gone! I'm sure this is some type of a dream, I bet I'm going to wake up and look outside and Mum will be opening the gate coming back from work.' Sarah continues to ponder in her thought.

'We haven't been back home for almost four weeks as we are still at Grandmas place. Oh goodness me, this isn't a nightmare, this is bloody real,' Sarah wipes a sudden dash of tears down her chicks.

'It's time for dinner', Grandma shouted. 'I'm not even hungry' Sarah thought, as she walked into her Grandma's lounge.

Chapter 2: *New Life & Life then, few months after.*

Sarah is still sitting by her swing chair, absent mindedly watching her kids who are chasing each other playing tag, she continues to remember her past in a wandered state.

Her mind hopped back to a few months after her Mum's passing.

'Okay! Okay! Gees! I will reduce the volume and for goodness sake, but can you please stop acting like you're Mum, because you are not!' Sarah angrily and impolitely surrendered to her extremely annoyed older sister's order; to reduce the loud volume from the radio which she had been blasting nonstop on repeat, listening to her favourite; Whitney Houston's *I will always love you*.

'Phew! finally, some peace and quiet' as Nancy stomped off to the next room.

Yes, the girls were no longer at Grandma's house, this was at their new rented home, in Braesideville a medium density suburb, quite similar in size and population to where their Mum's house was, Southertonville, a cozy small suburb, between Lochinville and the Industrial sites that connected to the West side of the City Centre.

Sarah and Nancy had just moved into their new place they now called home, where they had to pay rent. This supposed idea came along after this was suggested to them by their Mother's oldest brother, Uncle Dane, who actively helped them to navigate their suddenly changed life and lifestyle from thereon.

Meanwhile, little did they know that this new lifestyle change was not just going to be trivial, a tiny change at the surface, it was going to be so drastic that if it were a person, he or she would have felt like that guy in 'Get Out' movie where he was dreaming of falling into a sunken hole that never ended, and no one could hear his screams, taking him to another level of despair; that kind of change.

There was nothing else the girls could have done except for taking each dreadful day as it comes while they were waiting for their Mum's death estate to be calculated and finalized. Uncle Dane suggested that Sarah and Nancy rent out their own residential home so that they could generate a monthly income for themselves, enough to look after them, pay rent, buy groceries, pay for school fees and bus fares for getting to school and getting around. That sounded doable or so it seemed.

Uncle Dane introduced the girls to the contact person who was handling their Mom's estate at the Revenue department. Meetings were held and everyone got to know each other and discussed the process and what it entailed.

'All assets will be frozen as you already know, her Bank accounts will not be accessible to anyone, same applies with the Pension and Life Insurance until all calculations are finalized and all outstanding known and unknown liabilities, if any, have been paid and cleared. The government will then calculate inheritance tax and charge it off from her estate, any residual will then be given to you two, by default, being the dependents and heirs to her estate as stated on the Deed of Will. I hope everything is clear and understood.' The gentleman explained.

Then suddenly, Sarah's kids who were almost shouting on top of their voices said 'Hey Mum! Mum! Why are you not answering, can we get into the pool now, can we go in, please Mum?' Sarah was abruptly shrugged out of her deep thoughts as her kids were vigorously shaking her hand.

'Oh dear! Was I sleeping or what?' Sarah giggled as she slowly stood up and looked at her kids who were waiting eagerly for her permission to go into the pool?

'Are you guys ready to go in? Well then off you go, but please be careful when you dive in.'

The afternoon was still just as glorious as the kids splashed around in the warm saltwater pool. Sarah still grasping her glass of Rosé that she had not finished since earlier and she slowly sipped it, although it was warm at this stage.

As ugly as it tasted, she continued sipping on it as she does not believe in throwing away any food, a principle that was instilled into her whilst still young by her Grandma.

'Never throw away food, never throw away your blessings that God has given you,' She remembered her Grandma used to say this whenever they left bread to dry out in her metal Bread Bin. Sarah remembered how awful the dry bread tasted with tea when Grandma insisted that they finished eating the dry bread first, before eating the fresh loaf of bread.

Sarah laughed out loud at the thought. 'Oh Boy! Those were the good old days, crazy but damn good.'

Little did Sarah know that the same principle she used to frown upon and hated doing, later turned her into a very conscious and mindful person, who up till now, never throws away food that is still edible. Each time she even thinks about it, or sees her kids being careless with food, she hears her Grandma's voice telling her to never throw away your blessings, and quickly finds herself sounding exactly like her to her own kids.

'Ok guys shall we wrap up let's start going inside, it's time to go shower and get ready for dinner.' Sarah ordered the kids.

Chapter 3: *Sunset Cruising & Sister Chat*

Her daring love for watching the sunset is something that Sarah has been fond of doing for the longest time. Her occasional sunset cruises with her husband Derek are one of her favourite things to do and each time she goes out watching the sunset, it gives her a greater sense of gratitude to life. She sometimes weirdly compares the feeling to like the universe is whispering 'baby I don't want to leave, but I have to go.' The same kind of feeling a new couple feels when they are about to say goodbye to each other, but they don't want the moment to end.

'Baby look how magical it is, I can never get used to this, it's almost impossible not to daydream each time, even more special when I'm watching it with you. It's such a gorgeous sunset, can you play something jazzy, like Kenny G, I want to feel the music in my veins.' Sarah suggested to her hubby Derek as they drove down the highway enjoying one of their many 'sunset cruises'.

Such a carefree soul, filled with so much life, her forever young spirit, energetic and captivating that's undeniably noticeable. Although sometimes she is misunderstood by others who don't know her very well, she always finds a way to win their hearts by her love-filled outpouring spirit. To her, this is her way of expressing it, showing gratitude to God who has greatly blessed her.

If there is one person you will hear giving thanks loudly, even to the smallest thing, is Sarah. But all that joy is sometimes short lived by the deep feelings of sadness of not having parents. It consumes her so much as she often finds herself attaching everything back to her ordeal with her sister years ago. And each time these thoughts sweep through her mind, she gets a somber moment that tortures her.

Sarah pulls out her phone and captures a beautiful picture of the sunset and sends it to her sister Nancy via WhatsApp, who apparently is also a nature lover.

A few days passed, and Sarah got a call from Nancy, to have one of their hour-long conversations, updating each other with just about everything. Although Nancy constantly complains that Sarah never stops talking, she enjoys the long conversations she has with her sister.

'I have just finished sorting out clothes in my closet, ironed a few shirts, everything is spick and span, Omg! the excitement!!' Nancy shares her joy, she takes pride in her slightly obsessive way of doing things, in almost everything she does, be it cleaning, cooking or gardening, you name it. The sisters chatted away and found themselves diverging back to their many childhood memories, evidently a joyous relief that it's all in their past but never forgotten.

How could they forget the events that shaped and sharpened them to become who they are today?

Nancy's mind is amazingly sharp, she never forgets anything, in fact, she remembers everything, so many events that transpired during their darkest times, she elaborates them vividly, almost to how the day panned out, it's unreal.

On the contrary, Sarah tends to selectively remember events as if her mind intentionally blocks some of the bad memories away as a coping mechanism.

'The other day, I found myself just ruminating on how life was back then, when we were living in that rented house in Braesideville, how we didn't even know how to operate a budget, let alone manage cash.' Sarah said.

'Of course, I remember, how can I forget such!' Nancy answered.

Those were the trying times for the two sisters, whom at this time were now facing new challenges in their life of having to learn how to simply survive, from day to day, month to month, not knowing for how long they were going to endure the dreadful anticipation for a better day.

'Gees!! Remember how difficult and long those days were, we literally didn't have anything left to eat in the house, almost around the same time of the month, about the 20th of each month, those were the days. We were literary scrounging for food, only surviving on mealie meal porridge with sugar for breakfast, lunch and the same for dinner.' Sarah added, painfully laughing at the thought, bursting into a cry at the same time.

'Yep! That was hard!' Nancy calmly acknowledged.

Nancy is evidently emotionally stronger of the two sisters, besides being the older sister, her calmer nature yet tough and no push over, and her mental strength, is what somewhat helped the two sisters to pull through, just to get by. Even so, back then, Nancy found herself developing survival instincts, wanting so badly to make it through, while remaining collected, she always somehow found a solution amid the most difficult of times.

Their inexperience at life itself let alone how to manage a budget to make earns meet, was their toughest hurdle to overcome. Although they would buy staple foods for the month from their rental income, perhaps not enough money was allocated to these staples, as the rest of the money was required to pay for their new home rent and utilities, the change was then used for transportation to school and back.

'But for some reason Nancy, you always found a way for us to survive to the next day, you carried us through. I remember that friend of yours from your school, who lived close to us, what was her name again?', Sarah continued.

'Oh, that was Kathrine, the one who had the mulberry tree at her house', Nancy recalled.

'Yes! That's her, I remember you would go to her house most of the times after school and you would eat there and once in a while, you would bring back a sandwich or whatever for me to eat, that was really nice of you I tell you. You were probably like 'if I don't bring something for that girl at home, she is just gonna eat the same old 'corn meal porridge' Haha, I can laugh about it now.' Sarah recalled with tears in her eyes.

'Oh! how about the day I found out that they had that big mulberry tree at their back garden, OMG! That was like heaven. I asked Kathrine for a plastic bag and I filled it to the brim to bring home for us to eat.' Nancy recalled bursting into laughter.

'Yeah! More like manner from heaven, it became our new hangout spot. I bet Kathrine must have sensed something was off about us. She must have suspected that we were always hungry or something, I wonder if she ever said anything to you. I vividly remember going to her house with you one early Saturday morning, and we went straight to the mulberry tree and they were in the house, probably wondering what our deal was at that time of the morning. Imagine waking up and drawing curtains, only to see two girls up in your tree at the back garden'. Sarah said laughing.

'Yep, that was questionable, but she knew we lived on our own so I bet they must have suspected that something wasn't right, although she never said a word to me.' Nancy added.

'School recesses were the toughest for me on days where I wouldn't have anything to eat. I remember my tummy would get awfully painful and would go and drink water. I would avoid my friends at the start of each school break, so that they would finish eating when I'm not there. Best day of the week was when I had cooking class, that was like heaven Haha.' Sarah said.

'I bet that was.' Nancy replied.

'I always looked forward to Vince coming over to visit us whenever he was in town. He would always buy us some groceries. That was amazingly nice of him to do, considering that he was still in University.' Sarah added.

Vince was Nancy's boyfriend then, now her husband, who resided out of town but attended University in the same City where the girls lived.

Sarah had a like-dislike, more like a Tom and Jerry kind of relationship with Vince, one minute she liked him and the other minute, she disliked him. Sarah felt that each time he came over to visit them, he would take her sister's attention away from her. At the same time, she enjoyed him coming over because each time he did, would bring the girls some food.

'He saw it all, I'm glad it's all in the past now. We survived my dear, listen, I have to go, Vince is waiting, talk to you soon.' Nancy ended the conversation and off she went.

Chapter 4: *Breakfast with Derek*

After a gym session and a shower, Sarah joined her husband Derek, who was in the kitchen making their breakfast smoothies.

'That was Nancy on the phone,' as Sarah walked into the kitchen.

'Oh, hope they are all keeping well on their side.' Derek said.

'Yep, they are all good, but you know what!' Sarah said and paused for a second, as she sat down sipping her freshly brewed coffee that she had just made. 'Each time I speak to my sister, most of the times, we end up going back in time, as if it's our therapy that we do without even knowing. Each time we speak about it, I tend to shed a tear, can you imagine, even after all these years, it's quite relieving actually, having to pour it out with the person I went through the dark times with, just reflecting back, you know!! Are you even listening to me?' asking Derek who had turned to the cupboard to retrieve some glasses for the smoothie that he had made.

'Of course, I am listening to you hun,' Derek confirmed as he poured the drinks and walked towards Sarah, hands her a glass of mango & banana smoothie and sat beside her.

'I'm saying this because each time I talk to you about my past, you sort of look like you are not interested or listening to me'.

'I'm sorry babes you feel that way, but go on, I'm listening,' said Derek as he heartily assured her.

'Lately I have been thinking exactly what that Bible verse in Matthew actually means,

Matthew 5: 4 (NKJV), that reads

Blessed are those who mourn; for they shall be comforted.

Taking my sister and I's experience, it surely doesn't mean that you literally get comforted by people, you know!' Sarah continued.

'If you hear it being read out, without having had an experience where you desperately needed help or comfort, one will think that the comfort they are referring to is guaranteed, in contrary, it's far from reality. The opposite is true in that everyone is way too busy attending to their own pressing issues. Not trying to put a burden on anyone, but people literally forget, or they just don't bother to check in on you. I suppose they just assume that everyone is fine as long as no one is complaining. Nancy and I, as young as we were, had to learn fast that we only had each other to lean on; we buckled up and faced our new reality'. Sarah said as she sipped her smoothie.

'Was your Dad still alive then? Derek asked.

'Well! Yes he was alive, but do you remember I told you that my Mother and Dad separated when we were very young, so he had his own family and my Mum had hers, but my Stepdad had passed away a few years before my Mum. What I remember is that our stepbrother Jay, our Dad's youngest son, used to visit us a lot, sometimes he would bring us some groceries. He used to tell us that Dad sent his love and regards all the time, so we were cool like that. I guess he had his own reasons, as when my Mum passed on, there were some talks surrounding the fact that if he were to actively start communicating with us then, it would have appeared as if he was only interested in the estate, so, I guess he just didn't want to cause any speculations and we respected him regardless.' Sarah explained.

'Oh, I see.' Derek answered.

Anyway, thanks for listening babes' as Sarah sighed, in what appeared to be exhaustion and slowly reached over to Derek for a hug.

She held on to him tightly and rested her head on his shoulder, a bit longer than normal. Derek knew he had to just give her that comforting shoulder she needed and softly whispered, 'I'm here for you babes, I love you.'

Chapter 5: *Lunch chatting with Romona*

Another fine day, exhausted from yet another gym workout, Sarah dashed upstairs straight into her bedroom, contemplating whether to sit in the bath or have a shower instead. The shower ended up winning and as usual, considering her lack of extra time, juggling between errands of picking up kids from school, her work and running a household.

She quickly dashed inside her toilet cubicle to ease herself. She closed the door and while staring at her blank door, she remembered the prayer plaque that hung inside her childhood's home toilet that read:

Prayer of Serenity.

God grant me serenity, to accept the things I cannot change,

Courage to change the things I can,

And wisdom to know the difference.

She remembers how she used to feel a sense of calmness after reading this each time she used the bathroom; and how her Mother would end up knocking on the bathroom door as she used to take her dear time in there, I mean, who doesn't take their time while in the bathroom, perhaps re-reading the instructions of the toilet spray bottle.

Laughing at her own thoughts, Sarah remembered why she used to take her time in the bathroom, 'I used to take off all my clothes just to use the loo, how weird!', she continued laughing at her old self.

Her drifting thoughts flipped to recall a day of when their Mother told Sarah and her sister Nancy, just upon arriving back from their Grandma's home visit, that she had encountered a weird experience in that same bathroom, where she literally thought that the whole house was flipping and spinning, and that the toilet was upside down and how scared she was to open her mouth thinking that she would swallow the toilet water.

'Oh, damn it' Sarah muttered. Knowing what she knows now, that if one has this kind of a roller coaster experience or the house seems to be spinning; that's a very common tale-tell sign and early signs and symptoms of a stroke. Most people who later suffer an aneurism have reported similar experiences.

The fact that their Mother was a practicing Nurse, may have known what having such dizzy spells meant, and the bizarre fact that she kept saying thereon that she knew she didn't have many years left to live, and directed the girls to which portrait of her they should use at her own funeral, still haunts Sarah, who was sixteen at the time, till this day.

'Did Mum know she was going to die?' that's the unanswered question Sarah struggles with.

Their Mother went on to have a Stroke shortly after that and of course, the girls used her chosen photograph at her funeral memorial service as she had directed.

It's been more than twenty-five years since her passing, but the pain-filled memories still linger on.

Meanwhile as Sarah finally finished taking her shower still ingulfed in these thoughts, she dressed up and headed to the lounge to meet up with her eldest daughter Romona, who was having her brunch while watching TV.

As she sat down to join her, Sarah noticed that the movie *The Bodyguard* was playing, and Whitney Houston was belting one of her songs, *I wanna Run to You*.

'The Bodyguard! I love this movie, and that song! Omg, it's one of those songs I've told you about that I used to torture my sister with, making noise doing my rendition in the house nonstop.' Sarah laughing as she recalled.

'The other day I was thinking whether that whole load of singing I used to do was my way of self-therapy, because each time I sang, I would feel so good and happy, sort of like a relief, as I don't remember ever getting any comfort from anyone'. Sarah recalls.

'Aw! really Mum! you never had any comfort? That must have been very difficult for you. Have you ever thought of seeking therapy, because I notice that each time you talk about your Mum, you seem to be still in pain? I don't know how it feels to lose someone, and I don't wish it on me either, but that must have been really hard for you'. Romona said as she pitied her Mum.

'Of Course, it was very hard and still is, the fact that she never got to experience any of our life milestones and achievements, the graduations, getting married, having kids and getting jobs, she wasn't there to attend any of that, can you imagine that!. Each time there was a celebration of some sort in my life, I've always had mixed feeling of joy and sadness. I remember my Mum used to look forward to either my sister or I's wedding day and she couldn't wait to wear the biggest hat and dance away as the Mother of the bride. Well her dancing wish never came to pass.' Sarah sighed.

'Aw,' Romona massaging her Mum's hand.

'You should have seen the way we lived our first year after she died, it was rough, I thought that life was so cruel and unfair,' Sarah continued.

'I can only imagine it,' Romona empathized.

'I remember one time, coming back from school, I was so hungry. The thought of having the same cornmeal porridge again for dinner was dreadfully painful. I immediately thought of my cousin Jack, may his loving soul Rest in Peace. He worked in a Fast food joint near where I got my bus to go home. We used to waive at each other whenever I walked past his workplace. However, this one particular day, it was different, because I was so hungry, I waited to catch his attention while across the road and waived back at him. I decided to cross the busy street and went right inside the Cafe and I literally waited by the corner to chat with him.' Sarah elaborated.

'So, wait, did he notice that you had come inside the Cafe?' Romona asked.

'Yes, he did, but he waited until he was free to come over towards me. To my surprise, as if he knew, he offered me some food to go and I happily accepted the overture and told him to put a bit more so I could share with my sister when I get home. I was so happy to get free food and he didn't even know how bad things were at home'. Sarah continued.

'Oh really! Were you guys not talking about how things were going? Romona curiously asked.

'Nope! we never openly told anyone, not even one family member knew how rough things were for us, I guess everyone just assumed that things were okay with us because we never complained.' Sarah explained.

'But why would you not say something about it, like this was too much a burden for you guys, don't you think? Romona stated.

'It was hard, but **we** were also very young and still mourning, it would have been nice if people reached out without us trying to impose ourselves on them, you know what I mean. And based off that we agreed to just live our lives and not bother anybody.' Sarah explained.

'I'm so sorry you had to experience such hardships at a very young age, that must have been extremely tough.' Romona stated.

'Yes, it was, oh well! Look, you need to rewind the movie,' as Sarah gazed at the Tv but also trying to change the conversation.

Chapter 6: *Current life; triumphs & challenges*

Juggling between married life with kids, and just like her sister Nancy, Sarah also has a very lucrative job that she takes pride in, her love for accounting started early in life and now that she has acquired not only a degree but also other professional qualifications, she feels accomplished in her self-actualization goals.

Work life brings out another great quality about Sarah, she has been told that she exudes vigor and strength and does not crack when under pressure, as if she enjoys riding on these waves, like they are Beta waves.

This morning, the work meeting had just started, and Sarah was getting ready for her own time to do her presentation. Her presentation was so convincing to the Board members that George, her own Boss felt overshadowed by her, as everyone keenly sat at the edges of their seats while engaging to her well-presented and clearly elaborated facts.

The meeting ended on a great note with many applauds directed at Sarah, to the much dismay of George, who by now was evidently unusually quiet.

As the two drove back from the Head Office, Sarah could sense the resentment vibes she was getting from George. Sarah instantly attempted to clear the thick air in the car by talking, which was met by several one-word answers. Sarah realized that the journey back to the office was going to be horrendously long.

A few days passed and the air between herself and George had gotten thicker, you could slice it with a knife. Each time Sarah went to Georges office, she would notice that he was a bit dismissive and not as pleasant as he used to be. This was unbearable for Sarah who was excited to discuss about their recently approved Project that they had pitched together.

She had been copied into the email trails that confirmed the Project approval to go ahead with the Business expansion, something Sarah was thrilled to discuss with George about.

The anxiety was driving Sarah insane, that she gathered courage, headed straight to George's office.

'Hi, can I come in. I hope I'm not disturbing you; I could come back later when you're free.' Sarah said.

'Oh! come on right in,' George uttered.

George is generally such a pleasant and lovely guy, intelligent, tall in stature, appears slightly less confident in nature, passive to say the least.

'I have just opened some emails from Head Office, have you seen them? I'm so elated about the news.' Sarah said with excitement.

'Yes of course, that's some awesome news indeed. Thanks to you for your brilliant financial projections, that was our selling point to be honest, good job! The Board of Directors has approved to release the offshore funds and the Project Management Team is now being put together as we speak. Oh! by the way,

Board has specifically requested that you oversee the Financial aspect of the project, they said they were really impressed by your business acumen.' George added.

'Oh, my goodness! I'm lost for words! beyond excited and overwhelmed at the same time. Thank you for the compliment, although we both pitched the projections. I'm so glad they chose me, don't worry I won't let you down, I will represent our team effectively. Will keep you in the loop on how things are going, and I know for sure that I will benefit from that critical and analytical eye of yours.' Sarah said in amusement.

These are the qualities that George loves about Sarah, although she portrays herself with so much confidence, he likes that she respectfully honors his position as her Superior. It was obvious that he was bombed that the Board did not pick him to oversee the financial aspects of the project, but he happily takes the credit for being involved in the selection of Sarah two years ago to join his Financial Team. He knew that he needed her to complete his team with her freshly acquired Chartered certification plus her noticeable strong yet controlled assertive aura that she exudes without even trying.

'See, there is one thing I like about you Sarah, you make me look good, you are such a strong team member, although sometimes I may not show my appreciation, I do value it. Don't ever change, always be yourself'. George stated.

This out of the blue unanticipated praise got to Sarah who almost broke down into tears. She smiled through it as she remembered to stay collected, calm and professional as possible as she gently responded. 'I'm humbled by your words George, and sometimes the way I orate, may mistakenly be taken as that I'm being combative or belligerent but it's never intentional. I've been told that I come across too strong and may make others feel less of, of which it's never my intent. I can't help but to think that this may be resultant of how I had to toughen up at a very young age. I always attribute that part of my character is based off my childhood, being forced to deal with tough life challenges. From deciding what to do just to survive, to choosing a career path, and to staying disciplined, to completing tasks because it's the only thing to do. There was immense pressure to prove to ourselves that we were conquerors and stronger than our situation. My sister and I had to toughen up after the passing of our Mum and later our Dad. Looking back as tough as it was, I hate to say that it taught us resilience and shaped our characters into the beings we are today'. Sarah emotionally explained.

Her hard-shelled character does not overshadow her sparkling wit and unwavering moral center, she is surprisingly the most approachable, relatable and very kind person.

'Thank you for letting me know the other side of you, no wonder why you are the person you are today! you are a go-getter, driven and sometimes I cringe at the thought that one day you will be coming for my job'. George jokingly lightened up the mood and they both laughed as Sarah went back to her office.

Well let's just say that this ending was exactly what Sarah needed as she ultimately got a listening therapy session and be understood out of it all. She was in no way going for George's job as he joked about it, but one can't stop being afraid of Sarah's zeal that pours out of her without even trying.

The rest of the day at the office went by as usual except for Sarah who was now engaged into the email threads and getting to know the rest of the assigned Project team members. You can bet that Sarah was back in her element, all involved and no signs of cracking under pressure in sight.

Chapter 7: *The Outdoor Run*

Saturday morning......

Battling with random thoughts flicking through her head, Sarah feeling restless, checks the time in the dark; its 7:06am, she realizes it was way too early to wake up. She gently closed her eyes hoping to enjoy a lie in; one of her favorite things to do. She reached out to snuggle Derek from the back and slowly drifted back to sleep.

About 3 hours later, Sarah was awoken by the sound of cartoons playing in the background, she checks her time and it was 9:55am.

'What a good sleep I managed to squeeze in' Sarah thought as she pulls out of bed and walked to the window to draw the curtains.

Gazing into her ever so perfectly manicured garden, and then up to the beautiful mountain skyline, blue skies decorated with white clouds, the sun rays seeping through, it was indeed yet another beautiful day.

'I'm so grateful for all this, what a beautiful scenery to wake up to, thank you Lord.' Overwhelmed Sarah thought as she realized how blessed she felt at that moment.

Debating what to do after she changes, whether to go for her morning run on the treadmill in her gym or an outdoor run to enjoy the glorious weather, either way Sarah was off to a great start.

Whilst brushing her teeth, she noticed some stains on the mirror and started to clean all the mirrors in her bathroom. In her closet, Sarah realized she needed to collect clothes from the laundry downstairs as she couldn't find any of her sports bras. Off she went downstairs where she met up with a pile of clothes that needed sorting and folding into separate piles for the kids to collect for their bedrooms.

Half an hour later back into her closet, Sarah found herself sitting on the floor with all the drawers open as she started reorganizing the clothes. She has a, how should I put it, 'close-to-an-obsession' fondness in folding clothes only in one particular way, they all have to face the back, including underwear and she derives pleasure and fascination in doing this.

Sarah realized that she has jumped from one adhock task to another and another in a matter of minutes and frivolously smiled thinking to herself.

'Hmmm could this be the reason why one of my friends once called me 'flighty', I constantly move from one thing to another.' Sarah thought.

At that time when Sarah's friend told her this, Sarah recollected feeling a bit offended, but now she is beginning to see why it may have appeared as such.

The closet was now spotless, and Sarah was satisfied to now go for her run.

Outdoor run it was, as she stepped outside and breathing in that fresh breeze.

Trotting away with her headphones on her head, Sarah realized her music wasn't turned on and was okay with it as she didn't want the hassle of stopping her already going jogging rhythm.

The ambience and the beauty of the scenery serenaded her and brought a nostalgic feeling as she recalled going on jogs around her neighborhood back in Southertonville before her Mum died, gaudily remembering the route from her house in Boyd way, going around via Orpen way, into Britannia road then Fleming Road, turning right into Appleyard road, then back up McNaughton road that swiftly lead into Sycamore then back to Boyd way, her home.

She remembered never going for runs when she was living with Nancy on their own, 'Of course I wouldn't have had the energy to run, considering the scarcity of food in our kitchen'.

Trying to dig in more into her memory, she remembered that her sister Nancy took up a job at a local supermarket near where they lived during the first school break, packing up the shelves with food and she hated doing that job, knowing fully that they didn't have enough food at home. She tried it for a few weeks before she decided to try other avenues of making money.

Nancy have always had an exceptional entrepreneurship mentality, even way before their Mum died. She once owned a camera that she used to capture her school mates' pictures with, and she would charge them cost plus markup after developing and printing them.

Sarah remembered how Nancy suddenly came up with a great idea to start sewing stuff to sell at the Flea Market, as she had seen her schoolmate's Mum owning a table at the market and the idea dawned on her.

The girls had gotten a sewing machine as their Christmas present from their Mum, their very last Christmas with her before she died few months after. The girls have always had a passion for sewing, hence why they got one. Sewing soon became their favourite rush home to do hobby.

The very same sewing machine was going to change the girl's life around for the better.

Without even understanding the concept of Market Surveying, Target Market or Product Differentiation back then at that tender high-school-going age, Nancy and Sarah took to the Flea Market to see what was being sold so that they had an idea of what to make and how to be different coming into the market.

They had an advantage of knowing what was on trend, one from being the same age group with their target market and having an awareness and understanding of what was being considered as 'Hot' from watching Music Videos, and Fashion Magazines, what girls were wearing.

Most girls wanted to dress up as Tony Braxton, SWV or Envogue, hence how the idea of making floppy hats, and drawstring handbags came to mind. These items were the 'in-things' and all teenage girls wanted to own similar stuff. During their market survey, they realized that there was only one guy at the flea market, who was going to be their competitor, who seemingly had no clue of how to make any of the items he was selling, besides they weren't even as close to the real thing seen on TV.

The girls even pretended to want to buy a hat at the guys Market, just to have that close perusal and analysis of the hat and realized that they could undoubtedly make a way better version of it. The girls had an advantage that they were excellent at sewing; a skill they both learnt in Primary & High School.

As Sarah jogged on, she remembered how the sewing project eventually started. It was yet another month of scrounging to allocate food, rent and transport money for the period, when Nancy convinced Sarah for them to start their sewing projects, whilst the demand for the items was still on trend.

Without any delay, the girls bought a big batch of suede fabric material from Brooksville Fabrics, enough to make a batch that was intended to last for a good while.

Sarah remembers Nancy cutting open one of her old school hats so they could use it as a pattern. Excited as they were, they enthusiastically worked for hours, with try and error, a few twigging and resizing, and managed to make an awesome prototype and out of that, they made a few pattern stencils.

They wanted their hats to stand out and decided to add a sewn-on rose on some of them, or a bow tie. The bags were way easier to make as they had an invisible stitch, only showing from the inside. In the end, the hats and bags looked immaculate as obviously expected especially after working with Nancy who has a slight OCD in perfection. She derived pleasure in unstitching all the hats or bags that had a crooked stitch, to the annoyance of Sarah, who then had to pay attention to every detail, to avoid Nancy telling her to do it again.

Sarah enjoyed her thoughts as she kept jogging when she realized that she had gone 4 miles without stopping.

'Phew! I'm jaded, let me turn and walk back home'.

This is one of her favourite ways to reflect. Happy that these thoughts didn't make her cry or sad, she started playing some music on her way back home.

Chapter 8: *The Subtle Joy*

Another day at the office.

Sarah's work project had just wrapped up after months of nonstop involvement, she was relieved and feeling accomplished. Most Directors are ringing up her phone or emailing her, one after the other, after they had reviewed the final report of completion that she had just sent to them ahead of the meeting that week. They all were expressing their joy and congratulating Sarah on how impressive she was with her overall Finance overseeing and Management skills, from planning to execution, to the numerous review meetings with the Team, material sourcing and ensuring that only the best Suppliers with best pricing, and quality were used. Overall the feedback was all positive and thrilling for Sarah, probably the best moment in her working career.

One would have thought that with such great news, Sarah would be feeling on top of the world, but surprisingly she was not.

To Sarah, suddenly the moment was dreadfully long, all she wanted was to just stop with the praise and move on.

Sarah posed for a second, thinking what's really going on with her. Most often she notices that she doesn't dwell too much in a moment to cherish the joy derived from the accomplishments she has achieved in life. She thinks that her joy should be short lived, as if she thinks that people just exaggerate compliments. Not that she doesn't acknowledge the effort she puts in everything she does, she just thinks there is more she must do and more to accomplish, hence the less satisfaction.

Fast forward......

Driving home at the peak of the rush hour, traffic is at a standstill, something that Sarah is used to, she knows it will take her an extra 30minutes on top of the usual hour to get home.

'Dammit, I should have left early'. Sarah muttered out aloud. Sitting comfortably in her car, Sarah suddenly had an aha moment, that she may be feeling down and off because she often feels that she doesn't have anybody to share her joy with.

And again, she feeds her mind with the thoughts of imagining what her Mum would feel in a moment like this, where she would tell her about her successful work accomplishment like today.

Her imagination doesn't stop there, she creates a picture in her head how it would have felt telling her that she is graduating or getting married or pregnant!

'Perhaps if Mum was around, she would have easily ignited my feelings of triumph, like what Mums do, but it is what it is.' Sarah sadly concluded her thought.

'Or maybe I should call Derek, I know for sure he is going to be happy for me, let me call him, since I'm stuck in this traffic jam'. She decided in her thought.

Hoping to catch Derek free at that time, as he is ever so busy in his own successful career. Coincidentally, the phone rings on her car Bluetooth and she hears, 'Hi Babes'.

'Look who's calling! I was just about to call you, how's your day been?' Sarah responded to Derek.

'It was good, busy as usual, I'm about to rush into my last meeting before heading home. How's yours been, are you on your way home?'

'It was a good day, I sent my last report for that project, and got amazing reviews, literally, from everyone. You know what that means, a big bonus for me! I can't wait. Somebody please roll-in the month end.'

'That's awesome news Babes, will pass by and grab your favorite wine on my way home, will definitely celebrate this weekend. Got to go, love you.'

'Love you too, see you soon, bye!' said Sarah.

It's not quite the excitement Sarah envisioned in her head, it's just not what she expected it to feel like.

Sarah tried to phone her sister, her phone rang and at that moment in time, she didn't answer.

'Oh well, I guess it's really not that big of a deal after all.' Sarah thought.

The traffic had probably moved about three blocks since the time she spoke to Derek, Sarah yearned to get out of the City and promised to leave her workplace way earlier tomorrow as she was jaded. She continued to entertain herself with her thoughts while the music was playing softly in the background.

'Maybe I should speak to somebody or perhaps arrange to go for counseling since I have never had one. Why do I feel that there is something more to the way I feel, I wonder if there is something wrong with me?' Sarah thought to herself.

'Hmm! Beulah! I should call her; she is definitely the right person to help me with how to get about this since she studied Clinical Psychology.' Sarah thought and immediately directed Siri on her phone to call Beulah.

Both excited to talk to each other, it's been a minute. Beulah listened to Sarah as she explained her reason for calling and acknowledged what Sarah had just said to her.

'You are not wrong to feel that way Sarah. Having said that, Frankly and ethically speaking, I wouldn't be the best person to speak to or give you advise, due to the familiarity we have between us, that may lead to a biased opinion, I'm sure you know the constraints I have. However, I can hear you out anytime as a friend and outside my professional walls, but I'll hook you up with one of my colleagues, whom you don't know, to set up a meeting with you, how about that? Beulah explained.

'That's perfect, let's do that.' Sarah excitedly replied.

Chapter 9: *The Therapist: Nice to Meet you*

Weeks later.

Feeling excited and nervous at the same time Sarah got into the elevator, wondering how her first meeting with Malik would go. She could only imagine various therapy-related movies she had watched like the emotional; Good Will Hunting, Mr. and Mrs. Smith or the scary Hannibal and kept her imagination running wild in her head.

At the reception, the Receptionist was eagerly anticipating her arrival, but before she paged Malik, there he was, coming around the corner.

'Sarah?' Malik approached with a warm smile that eased off Sarah's anxiety.

'Yes, Malik?' Sarah smiling and acknowledging as she walked towards Malik.

'Hi, I'm Malik! Right on time and am pleased to meet you.'

'Same here, Malik, the traffic wasn't too bad getting here.'

As they headed to Malik's office, Sarah walked past Beula's office and lightly tapped her door and waved at her.

'Stunning views you have Malik, I'm in awe,' Sarah exclaimed.

'Yeah? I don't know how I got so lucky to get this corner office; I can't stop pinching myself. Please take a seat right here. Water, Tea or Coffee?'

'Water sounds good, thanks.' As Sarah took a seat.

The therapy session started, and Malik began by asking Sarah about what prompted her to seek for therapy. Sarah elaborated various events that has often led her to think she needed to speak to someone about how she felt.

'When you say you feel lonely and have no one to celebrate with, may I ask you to explain what you mean, considering that you are happily married with children?' Malik asked.

'Yeah I know it sounds off right! I do have a family that I so cherish, and they love me too, but I often feel a void that they can't fill. Sometimes I think that no one, including my beloved husband ever understands where I'm coming from, when I vent my sorrows, he obviously can't relate, he has both his parents, and what a blessing it is for him'.

'What does that make you feel?' Malik probed.

'It makes me feel so sad to know that I don't have any parents, not in a jealousy way, but in a wishful way. How I desperately wish that my Mum would have survived her stroke and be in a wheelchair and just being there, alive, you know what I mean, I would have been happier'.

'I understand what you mean Sarah, however the painful truth is she is not here, and she is never going to be around. Have you ever tried to look at it this way and try and process it from that standpoint?'

'Trust me, I have tried, but I find it hard to accept, till this day, as many situations keep triggering my longing for her. I feel that my only connection to the world, that fixed connection, my root, that is supposed to ground us all, was taken away from me when I was young, when I didn't quite know how to deal with it, and up till now, I don't know whether if I ever dealt with it the right way'. Sarah elaborated.

'How did you deal with it?' Malik probed.

'I don't know if I did to be honest, otherwise I probably wouldn't be sitting here seeking professional help like this. I would have grieved enough, of which I don't remember ever doing. I would have gotten some form of comfort, of which I don't remember ever getting any. Maybe if I had done all that I would be feeling a lot better.' Sarah said.

'I want you to look back to see how you got on, even if you think that you didn't deal with your loss the right way.' Malik prompted Sarah to explain further.

'Reflecting back, I don't remember ever dealing with it or how I got on, everything was happening so fast, whilst still in shock and emotionally unhinged, trying to come to terms with the whole death, my sister and I found ourselves devising ways to make a life on our own. One can only imagine the emotional struggle we went through at that age which forced me to place my feelings aside to the curb, and I remember turning the pain I was feeling into anger. I remember trying to vent my anger at God. I know this sounds crazy, but they were so many times I would literally envision God sitting on a chair right across from me, and I would be talking to him as if he were a visible person I could see.'

'Hmmm!' Malik nodding in agreement.

'I would question his love for me saying things like 'You say that you are God and you claim to love everyone! So how come you have put us in this horrid situation, how dare you take away the people that you placed on this earth to look after us, and now look at us suffering, living like destitute, blind man leading another blind man into an unknown forest, with no one to guide or comfort us!' Sarah continued.

'Oh wow,' Malik said.

'Malik! I was livid, bitter and hated on God so much, I wished it was just a nightmare. I remember asking him one day that if he truly loves me, he should turn this ordeal into a nightmare that I would wake up from and it's all but just a dream. I would go to bed wishing for a miracle, wake up, and nope it wasn't a dream but just the painful new reality. I didn't know who else to blame except God, although deep down I knew that wasn't the right thing to do.' Sarah continued.

'Right!' Malik said in agreement.

'There was this little, tiniest fire in me that kept burning, a little faith hanging by the rope, that kept whispering in my head that maybe God is indeed helping us right now and I haven't paid enough attention to notice. I remember slowly starting to look at things differently, like s-l-o-w-l-y, and started appreciating little things like 'at least we haven't slept without eating, or at least we have a roof over our heads and have some Rental Income coming in, although not enough, but it was something to be grateful for. Phew!' sighed Sarah as she reached for some tissues at the table.

'I'm really sorry you had to go through all that. Are you okay to continue?'

Sarah nodded in agreement to keep going.

'Well, feeling angry is also part of a grieving process, it's very normal for some people to go through such. We call it the 'Venting and Angry stage', where a grieving person blames others or even themselves for what they are going through, it's part of the process. Speaking of stages, there is one that I haven't heard you speak about, the mourning, what do you remember about that? How were you coping, and did you have any shoulder to cry on? I want you to go back to the start. This process might take some time, I want you to take your time, you may find it easier to write things down and keep a journal, that way it's....'

Sarah abruptly responded to Malik 'Oh no, I can't write it down, too painful. I once tried to write everything down back in 2008, the worst experience ever'.

'Oh! If writing is too much for you, then perhaps you can try recording yourself whenever you remember some things that comes into your memory. That way you can capture the emotions as you feel them without any pressure or too much effort of typing. I prefer you do it this way so that the process doesn't feel coerced, it will be entirely at your own pace.' Malik explained and suggested.

'I will try and do that Malik, although I think I won't be able to, without having a break down. Each time I narrate my story I end up in tears and I hate reliving the pain, its unbearable.' Sarah responded.

'I understand. Can I take you back to your writing experience, you mentioned that you started writing about your trauma in 2008? Do you mind telling me more about that, what happened, why did you stop?' Malik probed.

'Yes, that was in 2008 when I just had my son, I was so happy, him being my first son. So, I thought that was the perfect time to write a book. I wanted to capture all the emotions and wishes I had of wanting my Mum to have witnessed this. My approach to writing this book was probably wrong in the sense that I was writing it as myself, and not as the Author, hence I struggled to go past Chapter 4, I just couldn't deal with the pain and the tears, so I quit. I remember having to explain and would lie to my friends, whom I had told about the book, that it was still in the works, hoping that with time they would forget about it. Luckily time helped, and they eventually stopped asking, it was too agonizing for me to go through.' Sarah explained.

'Oh! I see, I sense the pain you have, even today as we speak but I'm here to help you go through this difficult hurdle. Hence why my assignment for you is to start recording your thoughts for me, whenever you can, and send over all the recordings ahead of our next month's meeting. I want you to let go and vent out all your feelings, don't hold back. My goal is by the very end of our therapy sessions, is for you to have gone through all the different emotions of grieving, then hopefully we will get to the last stage of finally accepting that we have no control over what happens in life and be at peace with it.' Malik explained.

'Right on, I look forward to that, and the recording part should be easy for me because I often talk to myself a lot and so it shouldn't be an uncomfortable thing to do'. Sarah smiled as she agreed.

'It was lovely meeting with you Sarah and I'm enthusiastically looking forward to seeing you soon. I will send you all the details in an email.' Malik closed the session and Sarah departed.

Chapter 10: *The Project & First Signs of Hope.*

Sarah comfortably relaxing at home one Saturday afternoon, slowly drifted into the memories of when they were living alone. She remembered the amount of work and time they had to put into their sewing project, days before launching.

The girls worked tirelessly that week to finish their first batch in time for their market launch on the coming Saturday.

The word had already spread amongst their school friends to come visit their Market stand and in no time, familiar faces were flooding their table in support and buying items from them. To their disbelief on how this idea was slowly becoming a fruitful money-making sensation.

The new battle was how they were going to keep up with the market demand without wearing themselves out, considering that they were both still in school. Something had to give. Nancy who was taking her Form 6 Science courses, a prerequisite to enter into Med School, on her pursuit to become a Doctor, found herself diverting more hours to the sewing project to the detriment of her study time. The right choice at that time was survival and as you can imagine, the study time suffered. Many trips were made back and forth to the Fabric Factory to buy more material for their business.

City girls were flocking their Market and for the first time the girls were sighing some relief and they could afford to reward themselves with some take away meals after each busy long day at the Market. Money steadily began to trickle in, but cautiously the girls understood that not all that money was profit, as some was working capital that needed to be rolled back into business, for buying more materials and paying for other expenses, the remaining was profit.

'We should employ someone who should work at our market table during the week, so that we can have more time to making more items.' Nancy suggested and in no time, they hired a widowed lady with an infant, who was recommended to them and she happily took the job while the girls got busy.

Many months passed, and the girls had gotten into the groove of running their small business. The stress and the hecticness of things were the order of the day but they rode on like true troopers. One could not deny the admiration of the tenacity of these two, very determined to win no matter what.

As the final school exams drew closer, and the juggle between schoolwork and business was still an imbalanced scale, Nancy knew at this time that her passion had changed from wanting to become a Doctor and slowly gravitating towards studying Business Studies. She wrote her exams with a changed focus to go into Business school and never looked back.

Christmas time meant that this was going to be the girls first holiday on their own.

'At least we have enough money to buy food, we should spend the day watching

Movies.' Nancy said considering that Christmas day falls almost at the end of the month, which has always been the toughest financial time for the girls.

Holidays were never going to be the same again, no more fresh cut Christmas Pine tree, no more Oliver's music playing in the background, all those memories were still in the girls heads.

Sarah doesn't recall the girls ever emotionally comforting each other as they got on with life during that time, except for just being present and looking out for each other. As sad as their journey was, the girls kept walking together, holding hands, pulling each other and never giving up.

Chapter 11: *Therapy Session 4: Welcome back*

'Wow Sarah! your recordings you sent me were pretty intense, I must tell you. I just liked how I could sense your emotions through your voice. What you are doing is powerful, in that it allows you to tap into your core thoughts that are buried in your mind and deal with them the way they affected you. Being able to revisit those raw emotions as painful as they sound, its self-healing and part of your healing process.' Malik said.

'Thank you for suggesting such an exercise, its exactly what I needed to do, quite therapeutic I found it to be. It made me look at my poor younger self in a different perspective and be able to give 'her' some credit, a thing that I have never thought of before. That 'she' was strong, a fighter and hence my persona today. This explains why a lot of compliments I get are about how strong my self-efficacy is, it's because I learnt from day one that I must believe in myself or be my own cheerleader and accomplish what I want to achieve in life. I find myself enthusiastically wanting to do things I have previously failed in doing before, like the idea of writing a book has crossed my mind a few times after we discussed about it last time. Not sure if I should pursue on it this time around.' Sarah stated.

'Oh! that sounds like an awesome idea.' Malik said in an encouraging voice.

'I have developed the idea you gave me of looking at myself from the outside in, by doing so, it has helped me remove the painful obstructions I kept getting the first time I tried writing a book.' Sarah calmly said.

'Interesting. I am glad you have found a coping mechanism, dealing with an obstacle full head on but directing it from the sidelines. I like that. So, tell me, how is that going for you? Have you started writing the book?' Malik asked.

'Like I said it's still an idea in my head. Maybe I should find an established Author who is willing to write it for me. I'm sure it will be easy for them as my recordings are well detailed. Each recording can pause as its own chapter and since the recordings describes the actual places where the event took place, just like my Therapy sessions with you like these, the writing and ideology would be easy to expand on to make it into a complete chapter. I hope you won't mind me including my Sessions with you in the book. Anyway, you would have heard all the recordings prior to sending them off to a book writer.' Sarah explained.

'Absolutely! Listen, I think that's a brilliant idea Sarah, can't wait to hear more about the book idea. I bet you will find someone reputable to write your book. I honestly don't mind being included in it, if at all, I'm pretty chuffed to know that our Therapy sessions will be featuring in the book, hurray!' Malik jokingly smiled as he adjusted his seat.

'Wait, don't get too excited now, I may record and paint you as the evil Therapist, and would ask the Author to label you as 'The Therapist from Hell' Haha!' Sarah playfully returned the joke.

'I would love that Haha!! Anyway, as I was saying, healing comes in different forms, like by talking about your experiences, journalizing your thoughts, or recording yourself like you have been doing. It's important that you take time you need to process or express your feelings, practicing mindfulness and finding an outlet to express your emotions; all these things help with the healing process. One's ability to emote, all depends on that person, there is no standardized or expected time to heal from trauma.' Malik said.

'I'm beginning to love coming over here to meet with you, compared to our very first session, where I was a bit apprehensive. I also can't wait to get the nitty gritty stuff done and get someone to write my book. Well for now I just have to find courage to dig deep and record all my thoughts and not to leave any stone unturned, wish me luck Malik.'

'Of course, you have all my blessings. Now, back to today's agenda, we are going to look at what we call Cognitive Behavioral Therapy. This is a...............' Malik chatted away as Sarah happily engaged, their therapy session continued and ended on yet another good note.

Chapter 12: *The Anticipation & The Setbacks*

As part of recording her thoughts as soon as she recalls them, Sarah quickly goes into her home office and closed the door, picked up her recorder and resumed as she remembers a stressful conversation she once had with her sister.

'I have just called our Executor and he is still saying the process is not yet complete. He says they are now paying all the outstanding debts, but they have run into some unforeseeable but not unusual financial problems. They don't have sufficient cash reserves left for the Inheritance Tax payment, which is the final part of the Death Estate calculations.' Frustrated Nancy explained.

'What does that mean? What is the Executor saying that we must do? What about the money from the insurance or pension, or savings he was talking about? Why can't they use that money? Sarah asked.

'Well, he said they have already utilized all those funds to pay off the balance on the Mortgage Account and that required a lot of money. From his explanations, it looks like all the money is gone but there are still some remaining outstanding debts to pay off'. Nancy sadly explained.

'So, where do they think we are going to get that money from? Ha! I can't believe this is happening. What is the solution, did he suggest anything? Sarah asked.

'There is only one option left, to sell the house and this has to be agreed by ourselves, as soon as possible, but it sucks. There is no other way to do this, the longer we take, the more interest charges will accrue each day on the outstanding dues.' Nancy explained.

'Wait, what? We need to what? No ways! That isn't fair, haven't we have suffered enough, and now we are forced to sell our house, the only asset we have left? Where are we going to live? How are we even going to afford College? This whole thing is ridiculous, never ending problems, oh my goodness me!' Distraught Sarah as she painfully asked millions of questions.

'I have to get back to him with our decision agreeing to sell the house, not that we have any other choice, do we? There's no other way to pay off the remaining liabilities and all the legal fees.' Nancy sadly concluded.

As sad as the news was, the girls had to take it as given and accept it. Within the following weeks the house was being advertised for sale, and it was a waiting game from thereon.

For the girls, this was the sad end of their home and it's memories they have been holding on to, but at the same time, hoping in anticipation that the house sells as fast as possible. The rental income had stopped ever since the decision to sell the house was agreed, meaning that from thereon, the girls had to fend for everything themselves.

The girls decided to move into a cheaper 2-bedroomed apartment in another suburb called Eastleaville, closer to the City Centre making its proximity beneficial to walk to and fro to the City if necessary.

It was still difficult to make earns meet, even though the new rent was cheaper, there was no longer the rental income coming in every month. To make matters worse, the new apartment owner was very strict, who, by the 5th of each month, would come to meet the girls asking them when and why they haven't deposited the rent at the stipulated date. Things got extremely hard for the girls, with only their small market income to rely on.

'Thank God another long school break, I have to look for a summer job to compensate for our lost income'. Sarah suggested.

She contacted their Aunt Rose, who immediately agreed for her to come and help in her Clinic for a few weeks, which went on well and Sarah was delighted with the extra money. She later contacted their cousin Luck (may his soul Rest in Peace) who had a Management job at a local Dairy Company, he agreed to employ her for two weeks at their stand at an upcoming Annual Agricultural Show exhibition.

Every little helped at this stage and while Sarah was earning extra cash, Nancy was busy at home making the bags and hats, ensuring they have enough inventory to keep the market going.

The apartment owner got frustrated with the girls struggling to pay rent by the 5th day of the month limit and she ordered the girls to move out after serving one month's notice.

Chapter 13: *The Thieving Saving Angel*

The unexpected downturn of events, searching for a new place to stay, almost close to school opening, with school fees deadline slowly creeping, and no steady income to sustain them, was a complete turmoil for the girls. Immediately they started looking for a smaller apartment and decided to sell the extra furniture they had in order to raise money.

They were excited to have found an apartment available immediately 'for sharing'. Nancy phoned and arranged to prepay the deposit so that they can secure the place.

On the day of moving, they hired a van and the driver also assisted the girls with the heavy furniture lifting.

On arrival at their new place, excited Nancy ran upstairs to let the guys know that they were ready to come in.

'Hello, hello, hello! Is anybody home, hello!' vigorously knocking at the door, Nancy was beginning to feel frustrated wondering whether there was anybody inside.

A pleasant lady from the next apartment came out to meet Nancy. 'Hi, I'm sorry but it looks like there is no one in that apartment, there has been people looking for them earlier, they must have travelled out of Town.'

'Oh, hi and pleased to meet you. Did you say out of Town? Do you reckon? How so? They should be expecting us, we have a truck load full of furniture ready to move in today as scheduled. I hope they are around Town, otherwise we won't have anywhere else to go to.' Nancy explained to the lady in shock and almost losing it.

'What are we going to do now, we have nowhere to go at this stage, my sister is downstairs with our furniture as I speak. I have to go ask the van driver to see if he can agree to wait with us for a while.' Nancy said as she walked towards the staircase.

Moreen, the pleasant next-door lady, appeared very friendly and felt very sorry for Nancy, that she immediately decided to help her out. They both went downstairs, only to find the van driver and Sarah almost halfway off-loading the furniture onto the pavement.

Almost in tears, Nancy explained the situation to Sarah and the van driver, but he couldn't help. Moreen consoled the girls and like an angel, she offered to help them by temporarily allowing them to put up in her apartment while they wait for the guys next door to arrive. They moved their furniture into her own apartment and the rest to her balcony.

Little did they know that this amazing angel that came from nowhere was going to steal from them.

The girls left a note to inform the guys next door that they are in the next apartment waiting for them.

The next day, the girls got the anticipated door knock from the guys next-door. But the news they got were not pleasing.

'What do you mean the rooms aren't available yet? Is that why you disappeared yesterday when you knew we were moving in that day? Had it not been for this generous lady, we could have slept outside. When are they going to be available? Displeased Nancy asked.

'I'm really sorry about yesterday, there was an emergency out of Town, I do apologize. I didn't have your number, I was going to call you, but realized last minute that you didn't give me any. I was hoping you would call me, but you didn't, I'm sorry. The guy who was supposed to move out decided to stay at the very last minute and I can't chase him out. I have your deposit refund right here, please count it to double check if all is there.' The guy said.

'Oh, my goodness! Where do we even start now! Our furniture is all in Maureen's apartment, and we have nowhere to go'. Nancy explained in disbelief.

'Don't worry girls, after hearing your story, I can let you stay with me until you get a place for yourself. There has been a lot of apartment advertisements for sharing lately, so you should be good soon.' Maureen calmed the girls and offered to help them out.

Nancy and Sarah were humbly grateful and very thankful to this helpful stranger. How could they be so lucky they thought.

'Thank you so much, we will pay rent for the days we are in and for this inconvenience we have put you in.' Nancy said.

'Don't worry girls, you are like little sisters I never had, so please focus on looking for a new place for yourselves and just buy your own food, the rest is fine with me.' Maureen said.

The next few mornings, the girls would wake up early to go buy a newspaper by the corner store so that they could catch the early bird. Some apartments were available but too expensive and some were too far from the City center. But one fine day, they found a two bedroomed apartment, with an immediate occupation clause, meaning they would need to move in right away.

Excited about this news, Nancy informed Maureen, who was very pleased for the girls and offered to help them move out.

'Sarah, can I talk to you for a second.' Seemingly distraught Nancy led Sarah outside to the corridor.

'I can't find the money that I put inside the suitcase. Remember the guy refunded us the deposit and I remember placing the envelope in the black suitcase by the corner, under the documents porch, but it's nowhere to be found.' Nancy whispered to Sarah.

Are you sure? Did you check properly, all the corners? You may need to remove all the clothes and shake them individually, where would it go? We were here all this while.' Sarah said but wondering what could have possibly happened to the money.

'Lord please let me find it, please Lord. Okay let's go back inside but don't say a word.' Nancy said.

The girls searched and searched to no avail. Somehow Maureen started to act weirdly suspicious, as if she is suddenly shy.

Nancy remembered that when she put the money in the suitcase, Maureen was with her in the room, and she remembered her asking if she had twenty dollars to borrow her as she wanted to go to the corner store.

'I thought I locked the suitcase, or did I? Did Maureen steal the money? I shouldn't think this way, she has been extremely nice to us, there is no way. But what if she actually did?' Nancy started to have mixed thoughts about Maureen as she recalled the day's event.

Stuck in a dilemma of whether to not ask Maureen and avoid the risk of spoiling their newfound relationship with their saving angel, or just call a spade a spade, and question her whether she has taken their missing money. The girls decided to grab the bull by the horns and kindly asked Maureen the most difficult question.

'What are you trying to say? Do you honestly think that I would do such a thing, after all I have done for you guys, I can't believe how ungrateful you are? I'm highly disappointed with you at this stage, anyway I have helped you by choice and I can't wait to have you go on with your lives.' Maureen sounded displeased with the girls questioning her, which made it awfully awkward for the girls to take in.

'We are so sorry Maureen, it's just that we have looked everywhere for it and can't find it. That's all we have. We need the money to pay for the new place, without it, we are going to lose the apartment.' Nancy explained almost in tears.

'Don't you have any money at all? But you told me that you own a small business at the Market. What about the bank?' Maureen asked.

'We have no bank accounts, no money at all. We live on hand to mouth, the market business, has a very small return and if we were to use that money, we would end up with no working capital at all. We used to get extra income from our family home but like we explained to you, our family home is now up for sale, and any residue left after all outstanding debts are paid, will be ours. We don't know how much and when that will be. I can't believe we are about to lose another opportunity to have our own place.' Nancy sadly explained.

'Oh, I see, hold on a minute!' Maureen said, 'I can help you guys with some money so that you can secure the place, but you have to pay me back.' Maureen strangely offered as if empathizing with the girls story.

'We need the money like yesterday, we are meeting with our new landlord at 7pm, in two hours, but the banks have just closed.' Worried Sarah explained.

'Hmm let me see, I think I should be able to help, I have some cash in the house, I always keep some in case of emergency.' Maureen said.

'You mean you have one thousand dollars right now? Nancy doubtfully asked Maureen, as she remembered that the other day, she was asking her for some money.

Maureen went to her bedroom and Nancy immediately hinted to Sarah that they should follow her.

Maureen startled by the girls sudden and unexpected appearance in her bedroom, she dropped a somewhat familiar looking khaki envelope to the ground. An envelope that looked suspiciously familiar to the one missing, to Nancy's surprise, but couldn't utter a word to question it as she quickly pinched Sarah, signaling her of her shock.

'Ah! Look......, ah.... the.... the.... I mean err! my envelope just fell,' caught off guard, Maureen weirdly stuttered as she struggled to construct a sentence that she wasn't expecting to make.

Nancy still stunned from what she was seeing, just played along as if she was not shocked to have vividly identified her missing envelope.

'Let me get it for you.' Nancy said as she bent down to grab the envelope.

'Oh! No, no! not...the, don't worry, I got it', as Maureen almost fell off the chair, jumping to grab the envelope from Nancy, which was visibly written 'Deposit' on it.

'Ah!...... Err......,' That was all Nancy could utter out of her mouth before she withheld herself from saying anything more.

Maureen quickly said, 'Okay guys, let's go to the lounge so that I will count the money for you to see if it's enough. It's been a long time I had it up there for emergencies like these. I'm glad I can help you guys. You guys are like my little sisters, and please take your time to repay me back.'

Nancy still withholding herself not to react to this baffling event unfolding before her eyes. One can only imagine how confusing the feelings were in her head, battling whether to say something and risk losing the opportunity to get the money, or saying nothing at all.

Nancy chose the latter, as it outweighed the risk of losing the money and their freedom. What a sad situation to be in.

They got the much-needed money from Maureen, well, how shall I put it, their 'missing money' was back in their hands as a loan. The price the girls were willing to pay at this stage. 'Angel Maureen' happily helped the girls to move into their new apartment safely and far away from duping strangers like herself.

The fact was Nancy and Sarah now knew that this amazing person who had sheltered them for almost a week for free was no angel.

'Phew! Sarah! Can you imagine that Maureen honestly thinks we don't know what she did! I'm stunned at how someone can sleep at night knowing fully that they have wronged innocent, let alone desperate and grieving people like us'. Nancy said in relief that Maureen is gone, and they are finally in their new home.

'You never know, she may wake up one day with a heavy heart and surprisingly come by and tell us that she actually stole our money and that we don't owe her anything.' Sarah hopefully added.

'That will be nice, but if she doesn't, then this whole thing will overshadow her overall kindness to us.'

Chapter 14: The rays of light

The girls continued with their hustle, working extra hard to make enough money for rent, paying bills and putting food on their table. Living in the City center eliminated travel costs to and fro their market, a huge saving on their budget.

Then one fine day, after what seemed to be like forever, Nancy made her usual phone call to check up on the progress with the Executor who surprisingly shared some good news, that the house had gotten an offer within the expected price range. Nancy was told to make time to go sign off some bunch of papers to finalize the agreement of sale.

Oh, what a feeling! as you can imagine, relief plus joy mixed with pain of losing their home, and everything in between.

The paperwork commenced, Lawyers meetings, more paperwork and finally the payment was made to the Executor, who then deducted all the remaining outstanding debts and the residue was now available to be handed over to the girls.

The girls were asked to come collect their cheque, but Nancy who at this time was taking some Aptitude tests, a prerequisite entry test requirement to study a

Computer Programming Course. She couldn't go herself and so she directed Sarah on a 3-hour bus ride to collect the cheque from the Executor's out of town situated office.

Holding on to the cheque for her dear life, Sarah kept her cool as she rode back home to meet her sister. The bus ride was long and when anyone was looking her way, Sarah thought they were suspicious, and she remembered her sister telling her to keep calm and look the other way and ensures she brings that cheque home.

As the door opened, instead of a somewhat joyful moment, as one would think, the girls shared a rather subdued moment, as Sarah handed over the cheque to Nancy, then hugged tightly, crying and shaking, overwhelmed with this sudden windfall of money in their hands and to their names.

Understanding fully that this money meant they no longer have a home; and this is the only remaining financial assistance they could ever have; and each decision they make from thereon, will determine their future. Quite a fast heart beating moment, but the girls did not panic.

The next day, the girls went to the Bank to meet up with a Bank Manager as advised by their Executor, so that they could open separate Bank Accounts to deposit their money.

The new struggle started hereon, on how they were going to manage the funds going forth.

Nancy, who by now had been accepted into her Computer Programming school, she was pleased to walk up to the Administration office to pay up the balance for her course fees in full, as she remembered how she had struggled to come up with the deposit to secure the place. Thanks to their Market business that helped with this process.

Meanwhile, Sarah still had few more months to complete her last semester in High School before she followed suit and registered into the same Computer Programming Course. The benefit of this Course was that as soon as completion, all students were guaranteed an automatic placement into jobs.

Nancy and Sarah took the free financial and career advice they got from their Executor to heart, that they should undertake fast-tracked career courses or diplomas with a maximum of one yearlong, those that can get them into the workforce fast enough, such that they won't have to heavily rely on their bank balances for their day to day living for too long.

Of course, the first thing the girls did was to pay back Maureen's supposed loan back, which she gladly accepted. Looking back, the girls never held any animosity towards her as they were thankful for her kindness, regardless of her short coming. She may have needed cash but the way she went about it wasn't right. The fact that she decided to still help them when they needed the cash was still kind of her to do.

Weeks passed and then Sarah remembered one clause in their Mum's Deeds of Will, that specified that a third of her Savings or Pension money was to be given to her parents if they were still alive. Although this may have not been the same money she was talking about, since such money she was referring to was already used up to pay off the Mortgage, Sarah thought that either way, they should still fulfill their mother's wish regardless, with the money they have.

Sarah discussed with Nancy and the girls agreed to honor their mum's wish and they found themselves withdrawing a third of cash each from their separate accounts, knowing fully that their grandparents may not need this money more than they do, but they still did it anyway.

The girls called for a meeting at their grandparents house, took a Taxi and surprised them with this gift.

The grandparents were so touched by the girls gesture and the difficult decision to honor their Mum's wish, considering that they no longer have a family home, and may have perhaps used this money towards buying another smaller home. One may say that on that day, integrity was unconsciously born by the girls and so are many more blessings that followed them.

During that meeting, the girls discussed and organized with their Grandparents a Memorial Service for their Mum and went on to purchase a beautiful black marble tombstone, engraved with bible verses chosen by their Grandmother for her daughter, and it read.

John 14 verse 1 - 3 (NIV)

1 Do not let your hearts be troubled. You believe in God, believe also in me.

2 My Father's house has many rooms; if that were not so, would I have told you that I am going there to prepare a place for you?

3 And if I go and prepare a place for you, I will come back and take you to be with me that you also may be where I am.

The Memorial service, led by their church Pastor and Choir was such a beautiful yet solemn event, and the girls got to meet the whole family gathered for the first time after their Mum's passing.

Everyone went back to Grandparents house where they ate and celebrated in remembrance of their Mum, in this moment, the girls realized that they had survived and bet their Mum would have been proud of them.

They came out of this ordeal stronger and wiser but above all with integrity.

Chapter 15: The Working life & The Orphan title.

Many months had passed, ten months to be exact. The girls were doing fine, Nancy had since settled into her job, working in a reputable Company in their marketing department. After her successful probation, she was given a company car as part of her package. She also had registered into a local college to pursue a program with the Institute of Marketing Management.

Meanwhile, Sarah had just finished her Computer Programming Course and had just been placed onto her very first office job in the accounts department which she was thoroughly enjoying.

On the first day of work, while Sarah was being introduced to the Management Team, she met a young lady who looked very familiar; but at first glance she couldn't place where she knew her face from, but suddenly remembered that she was the lady from TV, a popular Television Personality, Tarry.

Excited to let her know that she had recognized her, Sarah gathered herself up, so she didn't appear all giddy, and calmly smiled and said, 'Lovely to meet you in person Tarry, you are awesome on Television by the way.'

The girls instantly grew a liking for each other, and a platonic friendship was born. Tarry would invite Sarah for many drive-out lunches and offered to drop her home several times and their friendship grew stronger and stronger.

Tarry suddenly recalled that she saw an open call for an Audition for new Television Presenters at the Broadcasting Studios, where she worked a few nights a week after her day job for various Television Programs, she quickly thought that Sarah would make an ideal candidate for such a position. Tarry suggested that Sarah should give the Audition a try.

'First of all, you have such a lovely presence which I know they will instantly notice and love, and you are well spoken. I could give you a few prompts and let you go over a few lines with me and see how you get along'. Tarry suggested.

'Thanks, I'm fluttered, but do you realize that I stammer when I'm under pressure, I don't think that will work for me.' Sarah said.

'Trust me, you will be fine. Okay here you go' as Tarry hands over a paper with some lines to recite.

'Pretend you are in the studio, with lights and a camera in your face and look right here into the camera and start reading, you should remember to look up and do it naturally.' Tarry continued.

Sarah stammered even just to say the Hello Intro but with time, she ended up being confident and was smiling and keeping her eyes soft and pleasant, of which Tarry acknowledged and hence confidence boosting.

Of course, when the Auditions were now undertaking, Tarry had put in her word to the Producers, who were eager to meet Sarah. On the day, Sarah wore a Pink

Jacket with a black camisole and black pants, stayed away from the whites and creams as Tarry advised her, as these colors tend to wash out on screen.

After three takes at the live Auditions, which took forever as they were many people who came for same, Sarah and a few other people placed in a separate room were informed that they were all short listed, and would be notified about the results within a few days.

And just like that, around mid-week of the following week, Sarah got the good news, she was going to be one of the three new Program line-up Presenters on National Television, and since she has no car, she would have a designated driver to come pick her up from work or home on the days she will be scheduled to air. She would also have a selected wardrobe with items to choose from, a Hair Stylist and a Makeup Artist to help her glam up each time.

'Tarry! I got the job, thanks to you, I'm so grateful and elated right now.' Sarah joyfully said as she ran into Tarry's office to inform her of her recent news.

'No worries, it was all you and congratulations and welcome to

Television presenting, you will love it and the pecks are awesome too. You get to keep some of the clothes you wear for free and the rest are sold at a huge discount.' Tarry said.

Few weeks passed and everything was going great for Nancy and Sarah, or so it seemed.

Then one day as the girls were headed over to their workplaces, and as soon as Sarah entered her own, she met a guy who remembered her last name, and he asked her whether she was related to the late Television News Anchor who had just had a car accident and that it was on the morning News.

Sarah froze, couldn't speak for a moment as confusion erupted in her head. She managed to mutter that yes, she knows him and that he was her Father. Immediately she went upstairs to call her sister, who at the time had also heard the News while driving herself to work.

Sarah went to Tarry's office to let her know of her sad news, which shocked Tarry as she knew Sarah's Dad very well from the Broadcasting Corporation, but had no idea that these two were related, as

Sarah had never mentioned anything about her well known Father to her.

Tarry realized that this wasn't the time to start asking why she had never spoken about him. She kindly offered Sarah a ride home so that the sisters could meet there and start arranging to go to their Father's house for the funeral.

As they drove, the hourly morning news commenced and this reconfirmed his death to Sarah's distraught, she couldn't wait to get home to meet her sister.

Upon arrival, the girls hugged tightly and cried, another sadness in their life, in less than 2 years. Their almost healing hearts had to reopen to mourn the loss of their Father.

It was at this moment that they realized that they are now orphans, no more parents to call their own.

Reality hit as they got to their Dad's house, that he was truly gone, people had already crowded with News cameramen surrounding the house.

This was the end of a somewhat comfort blanket the girls were used to, of hearing their Father's voice on the National Radio or see him on Television.

It was at this moment, that all the almost buried sad feelings rushed through their minds again, that they no longer have their childhood home to go to, and no more parents to attend any future ceremonies yet to be accomplished in life.

Going forward from thereon, it will be just them, to cheer each other as they continue with life as official orphans.

Chapter 16: The Worst is left Unwritten

Staring at the blank Recorder before her, unconsciously clenching her jaw and biting her lips, trying to search for thoughts that she thinks are still in her head, but still unrecorded, Sarah decided to call her Sister Nancy, who immediately answered.

'Hey Sis, listen, I have been doing some digging into our past AGAIN! and I think I have told you that lately I have been recording my thoughts, a thing that my Therapist suggested that I should do. I have a feeling that there are somethings I am failing to remember, there should be more, why can't I seem to think of any.'

'What exactly do you want to know about because I remember everything.' Nancy said.

Suddenly 'I'm having some conflicting thoughts about some memories, sometimes I think that I'm imagining things in my head, and not until you confirm the incidents. I remember one time walking in the night from the City Center to Braesideville, tired but carrying some pot plants, why plants? Do you get what I mean, so confusing memories?' Sarah asked.

'We used to walk home a lot of times whenever we run out of money, don't you remember? Those plants you are talking about, were actually yours that you got from Grandma's. You've always loved nurturing plants. That day, we walked home because we didn't want to spend the small transport cash that Grandma had given us, it wasn't much, but we decided to save it for bus fares to school instead. It wasn't the best idea to walk, it took us almost two hours to walk back to Braesideville from her house.' Nancy explained.

'Oh! wow! I get it now. I'm asking you all this because I have come up with a brilliant idea to turn all my recordings I have been sending to my Therapist into a book. I'm currently in talks with several Publishers right now, although I haven't decided on who to consider writing the book. I have been having an awful feeling like there are more events that transpired that I am forgetting about. You know me, I have a mind block on some of our memories back then.' Sarah explained.

'That's true, your memory has always been selective; you tend to remember some things and completely have no recollection about other things.' Nancy said.

'Well guess what! apparently there is such a thing called selective remembering, Malik, my Therapist confirmed it. They call it selective amnesia, although I'm not diagnosed for having it, I somehow know for sure that's what it is. Sufferers tend to lose parts of their memory mostly those caused by trauma or death of a loved one.' Sarah explained.

'Interesting! That sounds like you. It's like your brain shuts off from some of the memories that I know happened, but you never seem to remember them unless I rejig your memory or sometimes you don't even remember anything. It's odd, you always appear as if you're hearing a new story, the way you continue saying, 'Oh really! Go on, then what happened after that?' In contrast to me, I remember everything you talk about, all our experiences back then.' Nancy explained.

'Honestly, I bet they have a name for people like you, who remembers everything LOL. But seriously speaking, thanks to you Sis for being so patient with me and taking your time to explain or rejig my memory. Oh, you're so sweet, loving, and very very.......'

'.... Err, Okay, okay I get it, enough with your compliments.' Nancy jokingly stopped Sarah, who probably would have continued praising her sister to almost her annoyance.

'Fine! So, who else came over to visit us, I just want to make sure that I capture the full story as was, without any filter?' Sarah asked.

'Let me just say, some of these memories are best left unspoken, as some visits from certain people ended up not being as pleasant as they should have been, its best you don't remember what was said. Let bygones be bygones, let's just agree that it was a painful experience, no wonder why you probably don't remember some of these things, you were way younger and emotionally immature to deal with the horridness of it. I remember at one point you locked yourself in your bedroom and cried yourself to sleep. It made me sad, but I was also in the same pain, except I dealt with mine differently from you. You have always been more needy than me.' Nancy stated.

'Yeah, I guess, but that's so sad, anyway I do understand where you are coming from, let bygones be bygones. Thanks for the chat sis, speak soon.'

'Alright then, bye for now,' as Nancy hung up.

Sarah sat in the same position for a while and found herself staring blankly again on the same recorder before reaching out to start playing it back. Before she reached halfway through, she abruptly paused it; closed her eyes consumed in sadness, she couldn't continue listening to it, too soon perhaps, as she could vividly sense the sadness in her Sister's voice and more so her own.

Chapter 17: *The beautiful blessings*

Sarah and Derek relaxing at their home watching their favourite Netflix series.

'You have been working hard Babes, your work project is out of the way, so, I'm thinking about a nice getaway. I want to take you and the kids somewhere super relaxing and fun during this spring break. I should be able to take some time off too this period.' Derek suggested.

'Omg! Wait, really! That's so nice of you Babes. Have you any place in mind, where do you want us to go to?' Sarah responded, all chuffed.

'Any of the Hawaii Islands would be nice I reckon. We all loved Honolulu, maybe let's go to Maui this time around, I heard they have many beautiful family-oriented beach Resorts, what do you think?'

'Sounds awesome, but leave the hotel selecting to me. I'll start searching now, you know I'm pretty good at picking lovely spots, I'll leave the flights booking and travel itinerary to you.' Sarah suggested.

Here's to yet another one of Derek's personality attributes that Sarah adores about him, besides being an extremely hardworking person, Sarah loves his spontaneity. His witty character perfectly complements Sarah's giddiness and like two big kids, they are the best of friends, ever laughing at each other's jokes.

Before you know it, the family arrived at their vacation destination, an exquisite Seven Star Resort that Sarah chose. The rooftop Penthouse was like a dreamland, with its own outdoor jacuzzi and pergola bar by its porch, overlooking several pools and some impeccably trimmed gardens that led to the shorelines of a white sand beach by the Pacific Ocean.

Just like a dream, this is the life that Sarah is living, filled with overflowing blessings that she doesn't fail to notice, surrounded by her family, she gives thanks to God for his favor and mercy.

Her husband and kids are constantly reminded to never take things for granted, to always give thanks to God, and express gratitude each day.

Each morning they woke up in that paradise, the family would debate on which restaurant to go for breakfast and as you can imagine the overwhelming joy that Sarah especially feels, the abundance, yet a constant reminder of what it felt like not having enough.

Her gratitude everyday was evidently expressed by her generosity to the serving Staff at the Restaurants, where she would gratefully tip them off as her heart is filled with appreciation. Giving is what Sarah loves doing, as she never forgets her time in the tunnel waiting for a better and easier day.

Fast forwarding to now, a complete contrast, where life is smooth sailing for both herself and her big sister Nancy, clear evidence of how making good decisions over bad ones impact our lives. Even if bad ones were made, Sarah remembered being able to identify them and knowing fully what to do to rectify the situation.

As she sat by the porch with Derek watching the kids enjoy their time in the jacuzzi of their penthouse suite, listening to Derek narrating his childhood stories and days in University, Sarah was trying hard to imagine what that felt like and also having parents at that age.

'My days in college were completely opposite from yours. It was only God that directed our life decisions into adulthood. We were never derailed from not pursuing schooling, in fact, we went onto getting multiple diplomas, degrees and professional qualifications on our own guidance. I guess the drive was there knowing fully that if we didn't become financially independent, the available funds would come to an end and would become destitute, or back to scrounging. I looked up to my sister a lot and was copying almost everything she was doing or studying; and because of her good decisions that I reciprocated, I tagged along on the right path until I eventually grew my own wings. That was God, just protecting and guiding us through.' Sarah elaborated.

'Wow, such a completely different story from mine. Thanks to your sister though for setting such a good precedence for you to follow,' said Derek.

'True'. Sarah agreed.

'Oh, I must also say that your wings grew beautifully and now look at you flying'. Derek cheerfully raised his glass to Sarah with a wink.

'I still can't imagine what it feels like especially as an adult, to having your parents, what does it really feel like? I often watch you in awe and curiosity whenever you speak to your parents and I try to put myself in that picture imagining it, but I never actually envision it.'

'To me it feels normal and because that's all I know, I can't imagine the opposite, it must be very hard. Derek replies.

'Yep, it is, and although I would want to say I'm used to it, it never is so at times. I'm sorry if you may have noticed a few times that I may have appeared detached or disconnected and I end up leaving the room whenever you are chatting with your parents, it's something I am still working on with Malik, my Therapist. He said I may feel that way because of the sudden overwhelming idea that 'I am nobody's child, or no parent can claim me as their own.'

'But look at yourself now, you are being claimed as somebody's parent, how amazing that is'. Derek said as he squeezed Sarah's shoulder.

'I guess so, it is an amazing feeling, fascinating and satisfying to be able to witness childhood again through my kids eyes. Watching them enjoying their own childhood makes me happy. I have adopted an Authoritative parenting style, where there is perfect balance of nurturing, discipline and structure. Of course, I had to read and learn about the different styles of parenting, to educate myself about what would be the best approach into parenting. I honestly think that there should be some parenting schools out there because most people end up becoming or adopting their own parent's parenting style, some of which would have been a bit hard ruled.'

'You are doing a great job Mama, if I do say so myself'. Derek said in her praise.

'Thanks hun'. Sarah smiled as she is reminded how blessed she is to have such a wonderful and supportive husband, who most times doesn't understand Sarah's pain but constantly continues to notice the void she sometimes feels and quickly fills it up with warm embrace. What a beautiful blessing it is.

Chapter 18: *Adopted Mindset Now & the Future*

Sarah's thoughts today...

'Here I am, relaxing in my bathing suit by the beach at this beautiful Island of Maui, watching the waves dancing back and forth, crushing against the shore, listening to some alpha waves music, playing softly into my ears, uplifting my spirit, mindfully thinking about how life has turned out to be. With the help of Malik, my Therapist, after several meetings, filled with tears and wailing, I have slowly managed to come to accept what is, and be at peace with it and not dwell on what was.

I am blessed, alive and healthy, I have a roof over my head, food to eat, a loving family and an army of friends, and I'm in good spirits.

There are so many things that I'm grateful for, but the reality is that we all have so many challenges we deal with in life that could be minimized by us simply adopting a concept of being grateful. By reminding ourselves about what we do have, and rather than constantly harping on what we don't have, is the start and way forward. There are some good things still happening, if we look closely, we get to wake up each day and breathe, our abilities to use our minds right, is a blessing in itself, and that could be the only thing we may need to change our mindset.

Instantly, I feel like the sun just got brighter and the air got crispier!

Yes, death is a suffocating experience; and like what Malik said, 'it's either you let it destroy you, define you or let it strengthen you'.

I have also heard others say that the universe has no accidents; therefore, you end up getting into a place of acceptance and for some like me, acceptance may require external assistance from people to get there. In the end, everything happens the way they are meant to happen.

I also believe that our intentions create our reality, and that our thoughts create positive and negative energy we feel. Negative thoughts breeds negativity and likewise the opposite is true.

I remember watching one lady on TV and she said, 'my life my blueprint, I am the master of my destiny' and this stuck with me. Although I agree with her that indeed my life is my blueprint, but in my case, The Lord is my Shepherd -Psalms 23. To me, he is the master of my destiny.

......And finally, a letter to my Mother.

Dear beloved Mum,

In case you have been wondering how we got on when you left, let's just say we survived. We survived because of the strength and resilience you bestowed in us; and like they say, from the ashes we rose like phoenixes.

You were one of a kind, calm yet strong, your presence was powerful, hardworking and never complained, you taught us to never whine about anything but to forge on.

Each time I see eagles flying, I think of you, as if you are saying, 'Soar like an eagle my beloved child, Soar up high to the sky'. The hardest times have been the milestones you missed, all of them, and what a painful pity I feel for you. You missed everything! the graduations, the weddings, the grandchildren and great grandchildren, but tell you what, you would have been proud, believe me Mum.

Still orphans, just happier and content with life. Still hard working, just gratefully orbiting in our own little galaxies.

I'm thankful for life and the smiles that surround us, more so, I'm grateful to Malik, my Therapist, for pushing me out of my mental stronghold and encouraged me to build the valor to do things that I never had enough bravery to do, like this very moment. This instant where I'm still sitting here, relaxing in my bathing suit by the beach, somewhere in Maui, watching the dancing waves at the shore of the Pacific Ocean, with my laptop, just about to sign off.

It's been a therapeutic journey and what a task I eventually took upon me, and this time I fought through the tears and just like Malik suggested, that I 'look-in from the outside' and separate myself from young Sarah, and I did just that.

What an awesome feeling to finally finish my book that I started in 2008, thanks to Malik for all his help.

Love and miss you forever, may your dear soul continue to Rest in heavenly Peace.

Peace and love'.
Signed**, **Sarah

Epilogue: *The Pain of an Orphan The comfort and hope*

Understood by a few, being an orphan is such an indescribable experience in life. For many, losing a parent/parents may seem like there is no longer anyone in this world who loves you unconditionally or is as concerned about your physical and emotional wellbeing the way a parent/parents care.

Most people seek out parental opinions and approval, whenever something good or exciting happens, wondering if they would be proud of who they have become.

The reality of the loss really hits when Mother's Day or Father's Day comes, when you realize that you don't have one.

The sad thing is, most people would expect one to get used to their loss, move on and stop to feel the void, considering the time that would have passed, but what they fail to understand is that, love feels the same today and always, may feel apart in distance but never at heart. The heart continuously loves and longs for our dear ones every day as so many things triggers the longing. The void remains irreplaceable, the memories remain present, the difference is that you can't be with them or call them anymore.

Within my journey, I eventually came to understand that grief can hold you hostage, but until you realize that the key is on the inside of the cell, you can walk out at any point. Seeking help is part of unlocking that cell and then comes solace.

Solace comes from healing of the heart and peace of the soul, and only when this happens, you learn that life is not promised, and you begin to see how cyclical life and death can be.

Seeing how tragedy can paralyze oneself for so long, I'm tempted to ask, can one *truly* recover from such a tremendous loss? The mind may perhaps say no, but having faith helps me say yes. The Bible reminds us about God protecting his orphans. When you think deeply that you are still here and still surviving, not by your own doing but by God's divine mercy, and by knowing this, that's where the most comfort lies.

The Bible says:

Psalms 146: 9 (NKJV)

The LORD watches over the strangers; He relieves the fatherless and widow; But the way of the wicked He turns upside down.

Psalms 68: 5 (NKJV)

A father of the fatherless, a defender of widows, Is God in His holy habitation.

Job 29: 12 (NKJV)

Because I delivered the poor who cried out, the fatherless and the one who had no helper.

And with this consolation, along with proper healing, comes comfort, peace and acceptance.

Finally, a message to those that are blessed with having their parent/parents alive: Love them dearly, hug them a little more, cherish the times you share together, create beautiful memories.

If you are my friend, trusting I may have already reminded you of this, because the pain of having none is inconsolable.

Acknowledgements

As with everything that I have accomplished in my life, this book would have not been possible without the love and support of the following people.

My husband, *Felix*; my love and the most lovingly committed father to our kids, there is absolutely no way I could have completed this book without your valuable analysis and edits. Thank you for all your encouragement and support, for reading some of the chapters as I wrote them. For that, I greatly appreciate you.

My sister, *Candy*; Where do I even begin? Thank you for helping me write this story about two orphans, for being ever tolerant with my endless annoyance. Thank you for everything and the countless times you have spent helping me unveil and peel off the layers in this book.

And finally, my kids, *Tanya*; thank you for helping to keep me buoyed by your unwavering belief in my vision for this book. Thank you for helping me with the continuity of the chapters, the endless edits, corrections and rephrasing throughout the book.

To *Alicia-Tyra* and *Jayden*; your enthusiasm and excitement after reading the first chapter, cheered me on right through to the end. I felt like a 'Cool Mum'.

To *Missy*, thank you for understanding that Mummy was extra busy, and you would sit quietly with me in my office, while I work on this book on top of my daily work. Thank you for the little massages, hugs and kisses.

Bibliography: References

https://www.biblestudytools.com/

https://www.biblegateway.com/

https://www.bible.com/

NIV - New International Version

NJKV- New King James Version

Printed in Great Britain
by Amazon